CATS SET V
The Designer Cats

SAVANNAH CATS

Jill C. Wheeler

ABDO Publishing Company

visit us at
www.abdopublishing.com

Published by ABDO Publishing Company, 8000 West 78th Street, Edina, Minnesota 55439.
Copyright © 2011 by Abdo Consulting Group, Inc. International copyrights reserved in
all countries. No part of this book may be reproduced in any form without written
permission from the publisher. The Checkerboard Library™ is a trademark and logo of
ABDO Publishing Company.

Printed in the United States of America, North Mankato, Minnesota.
092010
012011

♻ PRINTED ON RECYCLED PAPER

Cover Photo: Photo by Helmi Flick
Interior Photos: Corbis p. 7; Photo by Helmi Flick pp. 5, 9, 11, 13, 15, 17, 18, 19, 21;
    Photolibrary p. 6

Series Coordinator: Heidi M.D. Elston
Editors: Heidi M.D. Elston, BreAnn Rumsch
Cover & Interior Design: Neil Klinepier
Production Layout: Jaime Martens

Library of Congress Cataloging-in-Publication Data

Wheeler, Jill C., 1964-
  Savannah cats / Jill C. Wheeler.
    p. cm. -- (Cats. Set V, Designer cats)
  Includes bibliographical references and index.
  ISBN 978-1-60453-732-1 (alk. paper)
  1. Savannah cat--Juvenile literature. I. Title.
  SF449.S28W44 2010
  636.8--dc22
                                    2009021148

Thinking about a Designer Cat?
Some communities have laws that regulate hybrid animal ownership. Be sure
to check with your local authorities before buying a hybrid kitten.

CONTENTS

DESIGNER CATS TAKE THE STAGE

Imagine having a pet that looks like an African wildcat. Now picture that cat curling up on your lap. Thanks to designer cats, you can have that kind of pet!

Designer cats are **bred** to look like a wildcat but have the personality of a **domestic** cat. One of the most beautiful designer cats is the savannah cat. It is a cross between an African serval and a domestic cat.

Like all cats, savannahs are members of the family **Felidae**. This family has 37 different species. The domestic cat makes up one species. Others include the big wildcats such as lions, leopards, and tigers.

Designer cats such as savannahs display the grace and beauty of wildcats.

AFRICAN SERVALS

The serval is a wildcat native to Africa. It is found in grassy areas south of the Sahara region. Usually, the serval lives near water.

Black and white stripes appear on the back of the serval's ears. This feature is passed down to many savannah cats.

This medium-sized cat has a golden coat with black spots and stripes. As an adult, its body is 32 to 40 inches (80 to 100 cm) long. It stands about 20 inches (50 cm) tall. And, it weighs about 33 pounds (15 kg).

The serval is well adapted to its native surroundings. Long legs make it a fast runner and a good jumper. A lengthy neck allows it to see over tall grasses. And, large ears help the serval locate its prey.

This wildcat depends on a diet of birds, **rodents**, and hares. In wetter areas, the serval also eats reptiles and frogs.

The serval is a friendly wildcat. It looks like a small cheetah.

Mix It Up!

Cats have lived with humans for thousands of years. Today's **domestic** cats are **descendants** of wildcats that moved into human settlements. These wildcats controlled **rodent** populations. Eventually, they became the lovable companions we welcome into our homes.

Savannah cats can be created by **breeding** a serval with any ordinary house cat. However, spotted cats are usually used. These include Bengal cats, Oriental shorthairs, ocicats, and Egyptian maus. These domestic cats help give savannahs just the right look.

Bengal cat

Oriental shorthair

Egyptian maus

Ocicat

SAVANNAH STORY

The first savannah kitten was born on April 7, 1986. **Breeder** Judee Frank successfully bred a male African serval with a female **domestic** cat. Another breeder named Suzi Wood named the kitten Savannah. Eventually, this became the name of the **hybrid**, too.

Savannah went on to produce numerous **litters**. Cat enthusiast Patrick Kelley purchased one of Savannah's kittens. He then worked with breeder Joyce Sroufe to further develop the hybrid. Sroufe became a successful savannah breeder. In 1997, she introduced the savannah cat to the public.

Today, savannahs are rare. That is because breeding savannahs is difficult. Mating a serval with a domestic cat is not always successful.

After mating, more challenges lie ahead. Servals carry their young for about 73 days. **Domestic** mothers carry their young for about 63 days. Savannah kittens are often born early by wildcat standards. So, they may require special care.

The savannah cat is named for the region where the serval lives.

Savannah Cats

Savannahs are some of the most beautiful, **exotic**-looking designer cats. Through careful **breeding**, they look like smaller versions of the serval.

The savannah shares many similarities with the serval. This **domestic** cat stands tall and displays a medium-length tail. It has long legs, a lengthy neck, and large ears. The savannah's coloring and bold markings also resemble the serval.

Like its wild ancestor, the savannah is athletic and enjoys heights. Its long legs and lean build make it a great jumper. Like its domestic ancestor, the savannah has a friendly personality and is easy to care for.

Still, savannahs require a lot of human attention. They create strong bonds with their owners. Savannahs get along well with other pets, including dogs. And they are excellent with children.

Savannahs love riding in cars!

BEHAVIOR

Savannahs have the home-friendly qualities cat lovers want in a pet. They are friendly, playful, and energetic. Unlike many **domestic** cats, savannahs like water. They may even surprise owners in the shower!

Some savannah owners compare their cats to dogs. Savannahs may wait by the door for their owners to come home. These loving cats will even follow their owners around the house.

Also like dogs, savannahs can be trained. Some owners report their cats can play fetch and perform simple tricks. They can even be trained to walk on a leash when outside.

Savannahs like to explore!

COATS & COLORS

The savannah's coat is short to medium in length. It lies close to the body. Coarse **guard hairs** cover a soft undercoat. Yet, spots on the coat have a soft feel to them.

Breeders are still working to develop this **hybrid**. Still, there are already standards for these cats. Savannah colors should be black, black **smoke**, brown spotted tabby, or silver spotted tabby.

A spotted savannah has bold dark brown to black spots. These help create an **exotic** look. Stripes run from the back of the head to just over the shoulders.

Some color variations are allowed. Savannahs can also have dark markings on a silver or gold to orange coat.

The savannah also has dark tear stain markings. These markings start at the inner corner of each eye. They run down the sides of the nose to the whisker area.

The savannah's fur has a slightly coarse feel to it.

SIZES

The savannah is one of the largest **domestic** cats. Its tall, lean body may make it appear even heavier than it is.

A savannah's size will vary depending on whether it is a male or a female. Males tend to be

Savannahs take three years to reach their full size.

A savannah kitten (top) and a serval kitten

larger than females. Male savannahs range from
15 to 30 pounds (7 to 14 kg). Females weigh
between 9 and 17 pounds (4 and 8 kg).

The size of a savannah will also depend on its
generation. This refers to how closely related the
savannah is to the original serval parent. The closer
the savannah is to the serval, the larger it will be.

CARE

As pets, **domestic** cats are generally easy to care for. That is true of savannahs as well. They can learn to use a **litter box**. And, they don't require a special diet. Savannahs do best on a high-quality dry cat food. They also need plenty of fresh water.

Savannahs are high-energy, active cats. Owners need to have plenty of toys on hand. And, they must take time to play with their cats.

Generally, savannahs are healthy. Still, they should regularly see a veterinarian to receive standard **vaccines**. A veterinarian can also **spay** or **neuter** savannah kittens. This should be done when they are five to six months old.

Many domestic cats live as long as 15 years. Servals have been known to live to be 20 years old. With proper care, savannahs should live long, healthy lives.

Savannah kittens usually learn to use a litter box before they go to their new homes.

GLOSSARY

breed - a group of animals sharing the same ancestors and appearance. A breeder is a person who raises animals. Raising animals is often called breeding them.

descendant - a person or an animal that comes from a particular ancestor or group of ancestors.

domestic - tame, especially relating to animals.

exotic - strikingly, excitingly, or mysteriously different or unusual.

Felidae (FEHL-uh-dee) - the scientific Latin name for the cat family. Members of this family are called felids. They include domestic cats, lions, tigers, leopards, jaguars, cougars, wildcats, lynx, and cheetahs.

guard hair - one of the long, coarse hairs that protects a mammal's undercoat.

hybrid - an offspring of two animals or plants of different races, breeds, varieties, species, or genera.

litter - all of the kittens born at one time to a mother cat.

litter box - a box filled with cat litter, which is similar to sand. Cats use litter boxes to dispose of their waste.

neuter (NOO-tuhr) - to remove a male animal's reproductive organs.

rodent - any of several related animals that have large front teeth for gnawing. Common rodents include mice, squirrels, and beavers.

smoke - a solid-colored coat pattern featuring hair with white roots.

spay - to remove a female animal's reproductive organs.

vaccine (vak-SEEN) - a shot given to animals or humans to prevent them from getting an illness or a disease.

WEB SITES

To learn more about savannah cats, visit ABDO Publishing Company online. Web sites about savannah cats are featured on our Book Links page. These links are routinely monitored and updated to provide the most current information available.

www.abdopublishing.com

INDEX